Bharatiya Katha Vaibhava - 3

(Stories for Children)

Shreedarshan K.

ZORBA BOOKS

ZORBA BOOKS

Published by Zorba Books, November 2021
Website: www.zorbabooks.com
Email: info@zorbabooks.com

Cover design© Dhiraj

Title :- Bharatiya Katha Vaibhava – 3

ISBN Print Book - 978-93-90640-94-2
ISBN eBook – 978-93-90640-95-9

Zorba Books Pvt. Ltd. (opc)
Sushant Arcade,
Next to Courtyard Marriot,
Sushant Lok 1, Gurgaon – 122009, India
Printed in India

I dedicate this book to my guru Swami Chinmayananda of Chinmaya Mission.

I also would like to express my gratitude to the members of "Naadopaasana Trust" for their support and encouragement in bringing out this book.

Preface

Stories form an integral part of our lives. Bharat is a land filled with stories which can inspire and motivate even those who have lost all hope and are in dire despair. Every lane of this land sings a song of a great achiever, every monument echoes the valour of our heroes, every manuscript written by realized masters provide a direction for the spiritual seekers. These stories which have been written for children have been taken from our immortal Epics, Puranas and History which provide ample evidence for us to feel proud of our Rishis and Saints, Kings and Patrons of our National and Cultural heritage.

This book is a small, humble effort to put forth such wonderful stories in front of all our young minds. I hope the young and old alike would enjoy reading them and would be inspired to follow the footsteps of their glorious ancestors.

Shreedarshan K

Content

1. Glory of Srirangam

The creator, Brahma, invoked and prayed to Sri Mahavishnu, the Supreme Lord, to reveal his divine and glorious form. Pleased with his tapas, the Lord manifested himself from the ksheera-sagar (milk ocean) and appeared in front of Lord Brahma, along with his sacred chamber or vimana called 'Pranavakara Vimana', signifying Om-kara. The most charming and divinely beautiful Lord was none other than SRI RANGANATHA - 'the Lord presiding over the world-stage'. Lord Ranganatha and the Vimana were borne by the celestial king of birds, Garuda. Adisesha's hood was the canopy over the Lord. Vishvaksena (Ganapati) was leading from the front. The Sun and Moon were present on either side of the Lord. They offered their services to the Lord by waving the white chamaras. Narada and Tumburu were singing the glories of the Lord. Rudra and the other devatas were chanting sacred hymns and Apsaras were dancing in ecstasy. The devatas showered flowers from the celestial spheres.

Lord Ranganatha told Brahma to install his "archa-form" (idol) in Satyaloka on the banks of the heavenly river Viraja and worship him strictly according to the Agama Sastras. Lord Sun was chosen as the purohit for the daily worship of the Lord.

After some years had passed, King Ikshvaku of the Solar dynasty performed intense tapas to propitiate Lord Brahma. Pleased with his austerity, the Creator appeared before him and granted him a boon. Ikshvaku asked for the beautiful idol of Sri Ranganatha and Brahma bestowed the divine gift upon him. The king brought the idol of the Lord and installed it in his palace in Ayodhya. From that day onwards, Lord Ranganatha, who was daily worshipped by none other than the Creator and Lord Sun, became the family deity of the Kings of the Solar dynasty. Sri Rama, an avatar of Lord Vishnu, born in the Solar dynasty also daily worshipped Lord Ranganatha, the royal family deity.

When Rama, Seeta, and Lakshmana were exiled in the forest, Seeta was kidnapped by Ravana, the king of Lanka. She was held captive in Lanka. With the help of Sugreeva, the Vanara king, Jambavan, Hanuman and others, Rama and Lakshmana crossed the ocean and reached Lanka. In the fierce battle between Sri Rama and Ravana, Ravana was killed. Rama, accompanied by Seeta and Lakshmana, along with Sugreeva, Hanuman, Jambavan, Vibhishana and the vanaras returned to Ayodhya after the war. Sri Rama was crowned the King of Ayodhya. After the Pattabhisheka ceremony, Rama personally gave away gifts to everyone and especially to those who had helped him in the war with Ravana. When it was Vibhishana's turn, the Lord gifted the idol of Sri Ranganatha along with the Pranavakara Vimana to Vibhishana. Vibhishana was overwhelmed with joy! His eyes brimming with tears, he received the idol of Ranganatha from Rama. While returning to Lanka, Vibhishana carried the idol of Sri Ranganatha along with him. En route, the Sun started setting in the western horizon. It was time to perform the evening prayers - sandhyavandana. Vibhishana looked down and saw the river Kaveri flowing below. He immediately descended to the holy place known as Chandra Pushkarini where Ananta Sesha was worshipped. He placed the idol on a sesha-peetam and went to the river to perform sandhyavandana. After finishing the rituals, he went back and tried to lift the idol of the Lord, but he was unable to lift it. The idol had found its permanent place of installation. Vibhishana was filled with grief. He prayed to the Lord with a heavy heart. Lord Ranganatha appeared before him and consoled him saying that he had long ago promised his devotee, King Dharma Varma, that he would come to his kingdom in the South and take up his abode at Srirangam, on the banks of the holy river, Kaveri. The Lord was only fulfilling the promise given to his devotee, and Vibhishana was instrumental in fulfilling the promise given by the Lord to the king.

Lord Ranganatha told his devotee, Vibhishana, not to be disheartened. The Lord consoled him and told him that though his abode would be Srirangam, he would face South sending his divine grace and blessings to Vibhishana constantly. At Srirangam, Lord Ranganatha who reclines on the serpent-bed, is facing the South. His back is turned towards the North, his crown towards the West, and his feet towards the East. The sanctum, as well as the main entrance of the temple, also face the South - unique and rare!

The Lord told Vibhishana that he could visit Srirangam daily and offer his prayers to the Lord in the sanctum at midnight and return to Lanka in the morning. Andal, one of the greatest of the Alwar Saints, chose Sri Ranganatha as her divine bridegroom. In her bridal attire, she walked into the divine sanctum and merged with Lord Ranganatha. The arrangetram (first public presentation) of KAMBA RAMAYANA of the poet-saint Kambar and RAMA NATAKAM of Saint Arunachala Kavi were held in the auspicious presence of Lord Ranganatha at Srirangam.

2. Sri Vallabhacharya

Lakshmana Bhatta and Illamma were a pious couple who hailed from Andhra. They lived in Varanasi. They fled from Varanasi when there was a threat of Muslim invasion. At that time, Illamma was seven months pregnant. Due to the strain of travel and the fear of invaders, she gave birth to a premature child. The child did not show any signs of life. Totally heartbroken, they wrapped the lifeless child in a piece of cloth and placed it under a tree. Lord Krishna appeared in their dreams the same night and told them that he himself had taken birth as their child. Shocked and surprised, they both rushed to the spot where they had left the child. They were amazed to find the baby alive, protected by a ring of fire. The mother immediately put her hands through the fire-ring and took the child. The divine child was named Vallabha, which means 'Dear One' in Sanskrit.

Vallabha began his education when he was seven. He mastered the Vedas, the philosophies of Adi Sankaracharya, Madhvacharya, Ramanujacharya, Nimbaraka, as well as the Jain and Buddhist philosophies. By the age of eleven, he had completed his studies and reached Vrindavan. He was well known for his knowledge and was applauded by the scholars as 'Bala Saraswati'.

During his travels, Vallabha visited the Vijayanagara kingdom that was then ruled by the illustrious king, Krishnadevaraya. The king had summoned learned pundits and vidwans from various regions to discuss the various aspects of the philosophies enshrined in the Scriptures. There were numerous debates and discussions that went on for twenty seven days. Krishnadevaraya, who himself was a great scholar, was not satisfied by the various arguments and explanations given by the scholars assembled there. Vallabha, who was only eleven years of age, was summoned for the discussions and debates. After seven days of continuous debates, Vallabha won all the arguments. He was able to convince the king with his profound and vast knowledge. Krishnadevaraya was extremely pleased by the knowledge and clarity of thought of the young vidwan.

Krishnadevaraya performed 'Kanakabhisheka' for the brilliant scholar and offered the gold coins to Vallabha. However, Vallabha politely declined the offer and requested the king to distribute them among the learned and poor brahmanas. When the king lovingly insisted, Vallabha accepted seven gold coins in order to make ornaments for Lord Vittala in Pandarapur. The king, and all the assembled pundits, unanimously conferred the title: ACHARYA and JAGADGURU on Vallabha. Consequently, Vallabha came to be known as VALLABHACHARYA.

Vallabhacharya undertook an extensive pilgrimage. He recited and gave discourses on Bhagavat in eighty four places, which came to be known as 'Chaurasi Baithak'. All of them became well known pilgrimage centres. He spent four months in Vraja or Mathura every year. Once, when Vallabhacharya was meditating in Gokul, Lord Krishna appeared as Shrinathji and initiated him with the sacred mantra. In turn, he initiated his disciple, Damodaradas, with the mantra.

Vallabhacharya founded the 'pushti marg' or the 'path of spiritual nourishment' of Vaishnavism. Though he wanted to remain celibate, Lord Vittala ordered him to marry and lead the life of a householder and spread his teachings to everyone. The followers of the pushti marg worship Lord Krishna as Shrinathji, Mathuradeeshji, Dwarakadeeshji, Gokulnathji, Vittalanathji, Madanmohanlalji, Balakrishnaji, and Gokul Chandramaji. Vallabhacharya composed the well-known 'Madhurashtakam' on Lord Krishna, the Lord of Mathura. Once, Devi Yamuna asked Vallabhacharya to recite the Bhagavatha on her banks. At that time, he composed 'Yamunashtakam' in praise of her.

At the age of fifty two, Vallabhacharya took sanyasa along with the vow of Mouna (silence) and lived near Hanuman ghat on the Ganges bank in Kashi. He knew it was time for him to drop his mortal body. When the members of his family asked him for advice, since he had taken the vow of silence, he wrote on the sands. In three and a half slokas he wrote about 'unconditional surrender' to the Lord. It is said that the Lord himself came there and added another one and a half slokas. Together, they are known as 'Shiksha-sloki'. On the auspicious Ratha Yatra day, reciting the slokas attributed to the Gopis from the Bhagavat, Vallabhacharya entered the Ganges. Those who were present there saw a brilliant flame ascending into the sky. Vallabhacharya had merged with the Lord-of-his-heart, Shrinathji.

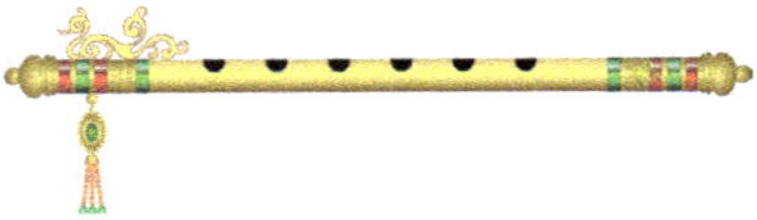

3. Tripurantaka: Destroyer of the three Flying Cities

Tarakaksha, Vidyunmali, and Kamalaksha were Tarakasura's sons. When the wicked Tarakasura was killed by Lord Subramanya, the three brothers decided to perform penance to acquire extraordinary powers and avenge their father's death. They undertook tapas, which included standing on one foot for a hundred years, surviving only on air for the next thousand years, and then standing on their heads for another thousand years.

Pleased with their intense tapas, Lord Brahma appeared in front of them and asked them what they wanted as a boon. All three brothers wanted immortality. The Lord told them that he could not grant them immortality because death is inevitable for one who is born according to the Laws of Nature. The three asuras discussed amongst themselves, and then asked for three flying fort-cities. A fort made of gold in the heavenly region to be ruled by Tarakaksha, a silver fort in the sky or intermediate space to be ruled by Kamalaksha, and a third fort made of iron on the terrestrial plane to be ruled by Vidyunmali. The three fort-cities were together known as TRIPURA. The asuras further told the creator that once in every thousand years, for a very short time interval, the cities would align themselves in a straight line. And at the time of alignment, if anyone destroys all the three cities with a single arrow, that would also be the end of their lives! Lord Brahma granted their unique boon!

Ruling over these flying cities, the arrogant asuras started tormenting the devatas, rishis, and beings on earth. All the devatas, along with Brahma and Vishnu, went to Lord Shiva and asked him to annihilate the asuras. Lord Shiva consoled and assured all of them that he would annihilate the asuras. Lord Sankara waited for the three flying-cities to align themselves in a straight line.

At the appropriate time, Bhumi-Devi (Mother Earth) became the golden chariot crafted by Viswakarma, the celestial architect. Brahma became the charioteer. Mount Meru became the bow and Vasuki, the serpent, became the bow-string. Lord Vishnu became the arrow called the Pashupatastra. All the celestial beings assembled in the sky to witness the destruction of Tripura. Lord Shiva waited with alertness and rapt attention. As soon as the three fort-cities aligned themselves in a straight line, which was hardly for a few seconds, the Lord released the arrow that went through all the three cities. The cities, as well as the three asuras, were burnt to ash because of the fiery astra. The day of "Tripura Samhara" happened to fall on Purnima, the full-moon day in the month of Kartika. Lord Shiva adorned himself with the ashes and came to be known as "Tripurantaka". The devatas were very happy. They came down to the ghats of the sacred River

Ganga, bathed themselves in the sacred waters, and celebrated the victory of good over evil by lighting rows and rows of 'deepas' (lamps). Hence, the Kartika Purnima came to be known as Dev Deepavali. It is also known as Tripurari Purnima.

The three cities represent the body, mind and intellect equipment of an individual. Lord Shiva destroying the three cities represents an individual transcending his body, mind and intellect and reaching the State of Enlightenment.

4. Lord Rama answers an Englishman's Prayer

Madurantakam is a small town in Chengalpattu District of Tamil Nadu. It has one of the oldest temples dedicated to Lord Sri Rama, which was constructed during the Pallava era. There is also a huge lake or tank in the town, which measures 13 square miles and 21 feet deep. It was built by the Chola kings. Colonel Lionel Blaze, a British officer, was the Chengalpattu District Collector during 1795-1799. He was in charge of Madurantakam as well. During his tenure, the lake breached twice and destroyed the dwellings and agricultural land of the people due to heavy rains. Blaze decided to camp at Madurantakam and construct a strong bund to the tank to save the people and agricultural land.

Lionel Blaze saw a large number of granite stones lying near the Rama temple and decided to use them for the tank bund. However, the priests of the temple told him that the granite stones were to be used for the extension of the temple complex. They were actually intended for constructing a shrine for Devi Seeta or Janakavalli. Blaze ridiculed them and said that it was much better to use the stones for the bund rather than the temple. He asked them, "Will your Rama come and protect the tank from breaching?" He made up his mind to use the granite stones for protecting the tank.

One night it rained very heavily. The waters in the tank were continuously rising. When Lionel Blaze was apprised of the grave situation, he immediately went and camped near the tank praying and hoping that the tank would not breach. But the waters kept rising. Breaching seemed imminent. At that moment, utterly helpless and in sheer desperation, he looked up to the skies and prayed to the Lord to save the tank from breaching. He also vowed to complete the construction of the temple. And, lo and behold! Wonder of wonders! In the brightness of lightning-flash he suddenly beheld two handsome and charming young warriors! They were standing on the tank bund and guarding the tank with bows in their hands and a quiver of arrows strapped to their backs! The rains mysteriously subsided. The tank was full and almost overflowing, but it did not breach! The people and fields were saved. Lionel was sure that the two youngsters who were on guard were none other than Lord Rama and his brother Lakshmana. Lord Rama had answered his prayers!

Collector Lionel Blaze was overwhelmed with joy at the Lord's compassion. As promised, and as a gesture of gratitude,

Collector Lionel Blaze finished the construction of the temple. The Collector's name is inscribed as a benefactor in the temple and the Lord is known as ERI KATHA RAMA - "Rama who saved the tank!"

Madurantakam is also the sacred place where Sri Ramanujacharya, the champion of Vishishtadvaita Philosophy, was initiated by his Guru, Periya Nambi. It also houses one of the most well-known Sri Ahobila Math Sanskrita Patasala.

"Sri Ramaya Tubhyam Namaha!"

5. Vidura's wife: Her Devotional Offering!

The Pandavas and their wife, Draupadi, returned to Hastinapur after twelve years of exile and one year of incognito. They claimed Indraprastha back, but Duryodhana was adamant that he would not let go of Indraprastha even if it meant a war with his own cousins. Yudhisthira, the eldest of the Pandavas, who was an embodiment of Dharma was not in favour of a war. He requested Lord Krishna to go to Hastinapur on their behalf as an ambassador of peace. The Lord agreed.

When the people of Hastinapur came to know that Lord Krishna was coming, many leaders extended an invitation to Krishna to accept their hospitality. Duryodhana sent a royal invitation as well, and arranged a lavish feast for Krishna. The Lord knew that Duryodhana's intention was to win his favour and have him on his side. Vidura, the great devotee of the Lord, also waited for the Lord's auspicious arrival. Vidura prayed to Lord

Krishna with devotion and mentally invited him to his humble home.

After reaching Hastinapur, Krishna directly went to Vidura's house and announced his arrival loudly. Vidura was not at home. Vidura's wife heard the Lord and ran to receive the divine guest! She saw the Lord smiling sweetly at the door. Overwhelmed with joy, her heart filled with devotion, she prostrated at his lotus feet. All these years she had heard about the divine glories and pastimes of the Lord. She had silently adored Lord Krishna in her heart like a gopi, all the time longing to have his darshan. And now the Lord was at her doorstep! A person who comes to our doorstep without prior appointment (thithi) is known as 'Athithi'. According to our scriptures, an 'athithi' who comes to one's house is the Lord Himself - "Athithi Devo Bhava". Here, Lord Krishna himself had come as the DIVINE ATHITHI!!

Sri Krishna walked into the house and Vidura's wife followed him - revelling in his wonderful lilas. Krishna seated himself comfortably on an asana and told her that he was hungry. She immediately ran to the kitchen and looked around. She saw a bunch of bananas lying there. She took them to Krishna and sat down at his feet. She picked up a banana and peeled the skin. Instead of giving the fruit to Krishna, she gave the banana peel to Krishna to eat and threw away the fruit. Revelling in the Lord's loving presence, she was completely unaware of her surroundings. Krishna who relishes devotion and devotion alone, accepted the peel happily and ate it. She continued

to give the Lord peel after peel and the Lord relished them all.

Meanwhile, Vidura was informed that Lord Krishna had reached his house. Taking leave of the royal assembly, he rushed to his house. When he walked into the house, he was shocked and stunned to see his wife sitting and feeding Krishna banana peels and Krishna happily relishing them all! She was so lost in her devotion to Krishna that she was totally unaware of what she was giving the Lord.

Vidura raised his voice and reprimanded his wife. When she heard Vidura's voice, she came to her senses. She realised that she had unknowingly discarded the fruit-pulp, while the peels had all been consumed by the Lord. She felt very embarrassed and ashamed. This time with all her attention on the fruit, she peeled another banana and offered the fruit to the Lord instead of the peel. The Lord accepted it, but he expressed his dissatisfaction. He asked Vidura why he had interfered in the "divine offering of devotion" that was going on. The Lord further added that the banana peel, which was offered with undivided attention and total devotion, was extremely sweet whereas the fruit offered with divided and distracted mental attention was tasteless!

Vidura understood what the Lord implied. The Lord, who is an embodiment of LOVE, seeks love and nothing but love from His devotees.

"Whatever is offered to Me, whether it is a leaf, flower, fruit or a drop of water, if it is offered with devotion, I accept it totally" ~ Lord Krishna (Verse 26, Chapter 9 - Bhagavad Geeta).

6. Narada's test of Devotion

Sage Narada was a great devotee of Lord Narayana. He was constantly playing on his divine veena and singing the Lord's name, and therefore considered himself as the best and greatest of Narayana's devotees. Once, he went to Vaikunta and asked Lord Hari who according to him was his greatest devotee. Narada was sure that the Lord would take his name. The Lord smiled and pointed to a farmer down below in one of the remotest villages and said that he was his greatest devotee. The Sage was shocked. He was the one who constantly chanted the Lord's name, day in and day out. Was he not the greatest devotee of the Lord?

Narada looked at the Lord questioningly. The Lord told Narada to go down and see for himself. Narada went down and quietly, unnoticed by anyone, stayed close to the farmer's humble and simple hut. Early in the morning the farmer woke up with the Lord's name NARAYANA on his lips. He went about his daily routine and later went to his field. He worked under the scorching

sun along with the other workers. He worked till late in the evening. He returned at dusk, washed himself, and spent some time with his wife and children and had his meal. Tired and exhausted, he fell asleep with the Lord's name NARAYANA again on his lips. The farmer remembered the Lord only twice during the day! Narada was confused. He decided to spend another couple of days there and watch the farmer. The farmer followed the same routine daily. Narada was quite annoyed. How could the Lord consider the farmer who took the Lord's name only TWICE a day as his greatest devotee? He rushed back to Vaikunta and narrated everything that had happened down below to the Lord.

The Lord smiled and told Narada that he would explain his reasons to him, but before that he wanted Narada to accomplish a task for him. The Lord gave Narada a pot filled with oil up to the brim. He asked him to balance it on his head, and go round Vaikunta and come back without spilling even a drop. Narada wondered what this had to do with his question, but he agreed since the Lord had set it as his condition for giving him an answer. Narada put down his veena, carefully picked up the pot of oil filled up to the brim, placed it on his head and started walking slowly. With all his attention focussed on the pot, Narada put forth his steps very cautiously and carefully and went round Vaikunta and came back. He was beaming with happiness since he had not spilt even a drop of oil while going round Vaikunta. He had been able to carry out the Lord's instructions completely and successfully.

Narada presented himself before the Lord and placed the oil filled pot in front of him gleefully. The Lord asked Narada how many times he had remembered NARAYANA when he went round Vaikunta. Narada was surprised and told the Lord that he had NOT remembered the Lord even ONCE. How could he remember the Lord when all his attention was on balancing the pot on his head to make sure that not a drop of oil spilled.

The Lord smiled and replied, "Narada, all that was given to you was a small job of balancing an oil filled pot on your head and going round Vaikunta, which took a couple of minutes. Yet, you forgot Me even during that short interval of time. And here is this farmer working day in and day out, shouldering all the responsibilities and problems of his family and work, and yet he never forgets to take my name NARAYANA, ONCE in the morning and ONCE in the evening". Hence according to the Lord, the farmer's devotion was superior to that of Narada's.

Narada immediately understood that this was the Lord's unique way of destroying his ego. Completely humbled, he prostrated to the Lord, seeking his forgiveness. He prayed to the Lord to grant him total and unconditional devotion, picked up his veena, and with "NARAYANA" on his lips left Vaikunta with a sense of total contentment and inexplicable bliss.

7. Lord Venkateshwara and Anantalwar

Sri Ramanujacharya, the great exponent of Vishishtadvaita Philosophy, entrusted one of his disciples, Anantalwar, with 'pushpa kainkaryam' - daily offering of flowers as a seva to Lord Venkateswara at Tirumala. Anantalwar happily accepted and settled down in Tirumala along with his wife. He would collect flowers daily, make a beautiful garland, and offer it to the Lord. Since it was not an easy task to collect the flowers in the hilly area, he decided to cultivate a flower garden. First, he decided to dig a well since a flower garden needs a perennial source of water.

Considering this as his seva to the Lord, Anantalwar took a vow that only he and his wife would engage themselves in this task and would not take the help of any other person.

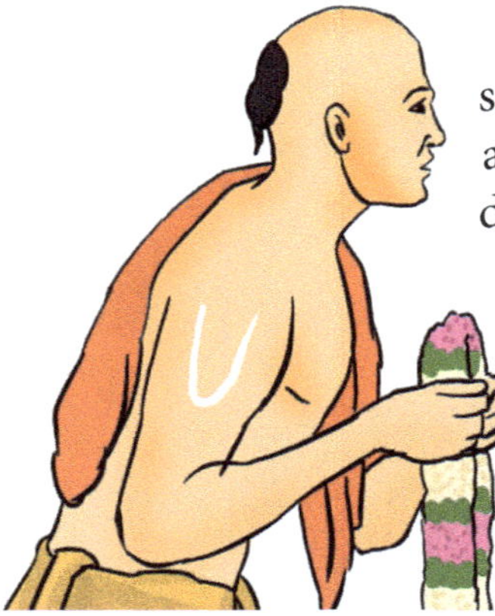

Anantalwar started digging the soil, loosening it, and filling it into a basket. His wife carried the basket downhill to empty it. She was pregnant and walking downhill and uphill was not easy for her. Nevertheless, she cheerfully participated in the seva. One day, a boy of about twelve years of age came along and offered his help when Anantalwar was digging the soil. Alwar politely refused, but the boy insisted. Anantalwar told the boy not to disturb him and asked him to go away.

The boy left, but soon after he approached Anantalwar's wife. He offered to help her. Not knowing her husband's vow, she readily agreed. The boy very happily helped in carrying the soil downhill. After some time, Anantalwar noticed that his wife was coming back faster to collect the soil! He found it very strange! Was she walking too fast? That was not possible. Was someone helping her? He decided to check. Anantalwar followed her unnoticed as she carried the basket of soil. To his utter dismay, he saw the boy whom he had sent away helping his wife in carrying and disposing the soil.

Anantalwar was furious. The adamant boy had disrupted his tapas. Seeing the angry Anantalwar, the boy started running away. He kept turning back to see if Anantalwar was following him. Sure enough, Anantalwar was running behind the boy, but could not catch him. In a fit of rage, he hurled the crowbar which was in his hand at the boy. It struck the boy's chin. Anantalwar tried to catch the boy, but he could not.

When Anantalwar went to the temple later the same day, the priests pointed out the Lord's idol to him. Anantalwar saw that the chin of the Lord was badly bruised and bleeding. He was shocked. He realised that the boy who had come to help him and his wife was none other than the Lord himself. The bleeding had to be checked. He looked around and saw 'pacha karpura' (edible camphor) in the sanctum. He took a handful of the karpura and applied it to the Lord's chin. Lo! The bleeding stopped. Anantalwar was overwhelmed at the Lord's grace and compassion. He prayed to Lord Venkateswara for forgiveness. The Lord appeared before him. Acknowledging Anantalwar's devotion and seva-bhav, the Lord declared that in future, his chin would be adorned with karpura every day as a part of his alankara, and without it, his alankara would be incomplete!

Since then, Lord Venkateswara's chin is daily adorned with karpura to remind everyone of Anantalwar and his devotion to the Lord. The karpura is later distributed as 'prasad'. The crowbar that Anantalwar hurled at the Lord can be seen displayed on the wall on the right side as one enters the main entrance of Lord Venkateswara's temple at Tirumala.

8. Narahari Sonar realises the oneness of Hari and Hara!

Narahari Sonar (13th century), who resided in Pandarapur, was a great devotee of Lord Shiva. He was a goldsmith by profession and was known for his honesty and sincerity. His skill and craftsmanship in creating the best jewellery drew a lot of customers from far and near. He often visited the Mallikarjuna temple nearby. Since he was a staunch devotee of Shiva, he refused to enter the famous Vittala temple in Pandarapur. He would not even look at the gopuram (tower) of the temple. During the festival time, he would move to a neighbouring village to avoid listening to the bhajans and keerthans sung by the devotees of Panduranga!

Once, a rich landlord and his wife visited Pandarapur. The childless couple prayed to Lord Panduranga to bless them with a child. The landlord took a vow that if they were blessed with a child, he would offer a gold waistband to the Lord as a token of his devout gratitude. The Lord answered his prayers and the couple were blessed with a child. To keep his promise, the landlord came to Pandarapur. On enquiring, he was informed that Narahari was the best craftsman in the town. The landlord went to Narahari and asked him to make a gold waistband for Lord Vittala. Initially, Narahari refused. But the landlord convinced him saying that it was he who was the customer and he would pay him well. Narahari agreed but on one condition. He would not go to the temple to take the Lord's waist measurement. The landlord agreed to get the same for him. The Lord's waist measurement was taken with the help of the purohit and provided to Narahari.

Narahari made a beautiful gem-studded gold waistband for Vittala and handed it to the landlord, who took it to the temple and handed it over to the purohit. When the purohit tried to put the waistband around Vittala's waist, he discovered that it was too small. It would not fit the Lord's waist. Disappointed, the landlord took it back to Narahari for rectification. Narahari was surprised. He had made the waistband strictly as per the specifications. How could it not fit Vittala's waist? Narahari worked on the waistband again and gave it back to the landlord. When the purohit tried to put it round the Lord's waist, this time it was too large! The waistband slipped down the Lord's waist! The landlord became impatient. He pleaded with Narahari to accompany him to the temple and take the measurement himself. But Narahari refused to enter the temple and have the Lord's darshan. The landlord suggested that Narahari could blindfold himself and take the measurement without seeing Vittala. Narahari agreed.

Narahari blindfolded himself and was led to the sanctum of Lord Panduranga. Narahari extended his hands towards the deity to take the measurement of the Lord's waist. Strange! When he

moved his hands over the deity, he suddenly felt that it was his beloved Lord Shiva in front of him. He felt the Lord's matted hair. His hands felt the familiar rudraksha and snake ornament round the neck. And around the Lord's waist it was surely the tiger's skin and not the silken robe! Narahari even felt a few drops of water on his hand - from Ganga who adorns Lord Shiva's matted locks!! How could this deity be Shiva, the Lord-of-his-heart? He quickly removed the cloth that covered his eyes and looked at the idol. But it was only the smiling Vittala who was in front of him. Rather annoyed, Narahari quickly blindfolded himself and felt the idol with his hands again. Sure, this time as well, it was the idol of Shiva and not Vittala! There was no mistaking. Realization dawned on Narahari. He now realised that Lord Shiva and Lord Panduranga Vittala are ONE AND THE SAME. This was all the Lila or Sport of the Lord to make him realize the essential oneness between Hara and Hari!!

He fell prostrate at Lord Vittala's lotus feet and begged to be forgiven for differentiating between Hara and Hari. Narahari was now a totally changed person. He renounced everything and completely dedicated himself to Lord Vittala who wears a crown with an emblem of Shiva-linga on it! Sant Narahari's devotion to the Lord is evident in the beautiful abhangs (kirtans) that he has composed.

Hara Hara Mahadev!!

Jai Jai Vittala Panduranga! Jai Hari Vittala Panduranga!!

9. Rameswaram - Dakshina Kashi

Sri Rama, Sita, and Lakshmana were almost nearing the end of the fourteen years of exile in the forest. Only a year remained until their return to Ayodhya. At that juncture, Ravana came and abducted Sita and took her away with him to Lanka, his kingdom. While searching for Sita, Rama and Lakshmana met the Vanaras in Kishkindha. Hanuman, the son of the wind-God (Vayu), crossed the ocean and found that Sita was held captive by Ravana in Ashokavana. Hanuman met Sita and spoke to her. He consoled and assured her of coming back with Rama and the Vanara army. Hanuman went back, reported everything to Lord Rama, and then they all proceeded to the southern-most tip of Bharat. A bridge had to be built across the ocean for them to move ahead.

At this point of time, Sage Agasthya came and suggested that Rama should worship and invoke the blessings of Lord Sankara before the construction of the bridge across the ocean. The Sage told Rama that Lord Sankara had promised that he would come to the South when Sri Rama invokes him. The auspicious muhurtha (time) was fixed for the pooja. Rama summoned Hanuman to his side and asked him to go to the Himalayas and bring the Shiva-linga from the abode of Lord Sankara. Hanuman immediately started off. However, he got delayed en route. The auspicious time was almost approaching. To prevent further delay, Rama made a Shiva-linga with his own hands from the sand on the shores of the ocean. The Shiva-linga was duly consecrated there.

Sage Agasthya officiated as the purohit and the pooja was conducted precisely at the appointed time. Hanuman returned with the Shiva-linga from Kailasa when the pooja had just finished. Hanuman was very disappointed that the Linga he had brought was not consecrated and wanted the same to be installed instead of the one made of sand. Rama agreed, provided Hanuman was able to remove the Shiva-linga that he had made. Hanuman immediately went forward, coiled his tail around the Shivalinga made of sand and tried to remove it, but it would not move. He tried again and again, and finally fell down totally exhausted.

Hanuman then realized that it was his Lord, Sri Rama, who had very lovingly made the Shiva-linga with his own hands. How could any might and strength dislodge it? Hanuman was completely and totally humbled. He prostrated at the Lord's feet and begged for his forgiveness for trying to remove the Shiva-linga, which had been consecrated and worshipped by the Lord himself.

Lord Rama consoled Hanuman and told him that his efforts

would be rewarded. He said that the Linga that Hanuman had brought would be consecrated along with the Shiva-linga that he had made. The Linga that Rama had made would be known as RAMANATHA, and the Linga that Hanuman had brought would be known as VISHWA LINGA or VISHWANATHA. And this holy place would be known as RAMANATHAPURAM - the Kashi of the South - 'Dakshina Kashi'. Sri Rama proclaimed that for the full benefit of the pilgrimage undertaken, the devotees and pilgrims must FIRST have the darshan of Vishwa Linga brought by Hanuman and only then offer worship at the altar of Ramanatha. He also stipulated that a pilgrimage to Kashi would be considered incomplete without Ramanathaswamy darshan!

"No one else is so dear to Me as Shiva. They who behold Lord Rameswara, surely on quitting the body will go directly to My abode. And anyone who performs abhishekam to Lord Ramanatha with the sacred waters of Ganga brought from Kashi will attain liberation and merge with Me. Whoever invokes Lord Ramanatha with intense faith and total devotion will be blessed by Sankara with devotion for Me (Rama-bhakti). And he who has a glimpse of the bridge (Setu) built by Me across the ocean will surely cross the ocean of samsara without any difficulty" ~ Lord Rama's words in Sri Ramacharitmanas by Goswami Tulasidasji.

"Those who have a glimpse of the Setu after invoking Rameswara will become free of all their sins by My grace. Those who take a holy dip in the waters of Setu, have the darshan of Rameswara, take a vow and then undertake a pilgrimage to Varanasi, bring the holy waters of Ganga and perform abhisheka to Lord Rameswara will be totally liberated from the bondages of samsara and reach the State of Total Liberation" ~ Lord Shiva to Parvati in Adhyatma Ramayana.

10. Karaikal Ammaiyar

Punithavati (6th Century AD) was a great devotee of Lord Shiva. She belonged to the merchant community and lived in Karaikal, Puducherry. She is one of the 63 great Shaivite saints known as Nayanmars. She spent her time glorifying the Lord and serving his devotees, especially those who came to visit the town. A wealthy businessman, Paramadattan, who was from Nagapattinam married the beautiful Punithavati. She devoted herself to household chores while continuing her religious duties.

One day, a relative of Paramadattan visited him at his work-place. He gave Paramadattan two mangoes from his garden. Paramadattan sent them to his house through his servant. Punithavati received them and placed them at the altar of the Lord. A little later, a Shiva Bhakta came along seeking for alms. Punithavati offered food to the sadhu along with one of the mangoes that her husband had sent.

Later, Paramadattan came home and sat down to have his meal. He asked for the mango. Punithavathi brought the mango that she had kept at the Lord's altar and gave it to Paramadattan. He found it extremely sweet and asked for the second one. It was not there. She had given it away as bhiksha to the sadhu. Knowing her husband's temper and not knowing what to do, she ran to the pooja altar. Her eyes overflowing with tears, she prayed fervently to the Lord to save her from the situation. As she pleaded with the Lord, a mango appeared in her hands! Overwhelmed at the Lord's grace, she quickly went and gave it to her husband. This divine mango was far more sweeter in taste than the first one. How could two mangoes differ so much in taste? Obviously, this was not the same mango that he had sent home. Paramadattan asked his wife to tell him the truth. Slowly, she narrated everything to him. He was stunned. With absolute disbelief, he told her to ask Lord Shiva for one more mango. She was reluctant, but he insisted. She went to the altar again and prayed to the Lord. Lo! Another mango appeared in her hand. She went back and gave the mango to Paramadattan. The moment he touched the mango, it disappeared. Paramadattan realized that his wife was not an ordinary woman but one of the greatest devotees of Parameshwara. He was filled with awe and respect for Punithavati. He no longer considered her as his mortal wife. She was his Guru who had opened his eyes. He silently left home and settled down in the neighbouring Pandiyan kingdom. He married a local merchant's daughter and even named his daughter Punithavati!

Punithavati's family located Paramadattan at Madurai and took her with them to his house. On seeing Punithavati,

Paramadattan who now worshipfully respected and revered her, immediately came forward and offered his salutations to her, along with his wife and daughter. The bewildered family of Punithavati left for their home not knowing what to do. Punithavati was now totally transformed. Severing all worldly ties, she completely and totally dedicated herself to Lord Sankara. Realising that her beauty and youthfulness were the greatest impediment, she pleaded with the Lord to take away her beauty and give her an old and ugly form. The Lord granted her wish! Suddenly, she became old in appearance and frightfully ugly to look at. Her frightful look brought fear to some, but evoked respect from others. Many beautiful and devotional compositions on Lord Shiva are attributed to her.

Punithavati wanted to have the darshan of Lord Parameshwara, and started her journey Northward to Kailasa. The moment she saw the divine Kailasa mountain, the abode of the Lord, she was reluctant to place her feet on them. She placed her head down on the sacred ground and started walking with the help of her hands! Devi Parvati was astonished at this sight, and asked Shiva who she was. Extremely pleased with Punithavati's devotion, the Lord addressed her as AMMAIYE (Mother), and told Parvati that she was a mother-figure to him! Punithavati became known as KARAIKAL AMMAIYAR. Lord Shiva and Parvati gave her darshan. In turn, Ammaiyar addressed the Lord as APPANE (father) and asked for mukti. She also said that if at all she had to be born again, she should only be born as his devotee. Ammaiyar expressed her desire to see Shiva's divine dance: the Tandava, while she sang for him. The Lord told her to go to Tiruvalangadu in Tamil Nadu, where she would be able to witness his Tandava. Ammaiyar proceeded to Tiruvalangadu where Lord Shiva is worshipped as Vataranyeswara. Ammaiyar sang ecstatically with a pair of cymbals in

hand, while Lord Nataraja danced! Of the five famous sabhas (divine halls) attributed to Lord Nataraja, Tiruvalangadu is known as Ratna Sabha - the Hall of Gems, where the Lord performed the Urdhva Tandava. Ammaiyar stayed at Tiruvalangadu, singing the Lord's glories. She continued her devoted services unto him till she finally merged with Lord Shiva.

11. Tyagaraja Swami of the Carnatic Music Trinity

Sri Tyagabrahma or Sri Tyagaraja Swami (1767-1847AD) is one among the Music Trinity of Carnatic Music. He was born to a pious couple in Tiruvarur in Tamil Nadu. Along with the study of Sastras, he learnt music from the well-known Vidwan, Sonti Venkataramanaiah. He was an ardent devotee of Lord Rama, and started composing keerthans at a very young age. The idol of Sri Rama was a living presence for him. Tyagaraja associated simple daily activities like waking up, taking a bath, eating, sleeping, etc., with the Lord and composed kirtans for all these occasions. He studied the Naradeeyam, a treatise on music. He considered Sage

Narada as his Guru and constantly and consistently meditated on him. Sage Narada appeared before Tyagaraja, blessed him, and bestowed on him Sangeeta Sastra (knowledge of music).

Tyagaraja was also initiated into the Sri Rama mantra. When he completed chanting the mantra ninety six crore times, he was blessed with the vision of Lord Rama accompanied by his consort, Sita. An overwhelmed Tyagaraja sang in praise of his divine parents: Devi Sita and Sri Rama.

After his marriage, Tyagaraja led an extremely simple life of a householder. Sri Rama was his wealth and Rama Bhakti was his kingdom. When the king heard of the great musician, he extended a royal invitation to Tyagaraja to become the court musician. He sent royal gifts in the form of silken apparel, gem-studded ornaments, and gold coins. Tyagaraja politely declined both - the royal gifts and the glory of becoming a court musician. He composed a beautiful kriti: "O Mind, tell me the truth. What gives you real happiness - material wealth or Lord Rama's divine association?" The royal attendants went back.

Tyagaraja's elder brother was very annoyed. He was unhappy that his brother had rejected the seat of Asthana Vidwan (court musician). He blamed it all on Lord Rama who had become the heart and soul of his brother. At night, Tyagaraja's brother secretly took the idol of Lord Rama from the puja-room and tossed it into the Kaveri river. In the morning, when Tyagaraja went into the prayer room for his daily worship, he found the idol missing. Overwhelmed with grief, for days he searched for his beloved Lord Sri Rama. He went on a pilgrimage, and at every pilgrimage centre, Tyagaraja composed beautiful kirtans on the presiding deity of that temple. After a long, arduous search, the Lord

appeared in his dream and told him that the idol that he used to worship had been tossed into the waters of the river Kaveri. Extremely happy, Tyagaraja retrieved the idol of Sri Rama and with all festive celebrations, brought it back and reinstalled it in his puja room. His brother realized his mistake and also understood the unflinching devotion that Tyagaraja had for the Lord.

During Tyagaraja's daughter's wedding, one of his disciples brought a beautiful portrait of Lord Rama and Sita as a gift for the newly-weds. Tyagaraja saw his disciple coming towards him from a distance. He was carrying the gift. For Tyagaraja, it was not just a portrait. It was the Lord accompanied by Sita walking towards him. With a joyous heart overflowing with devotion, he sang, "O Lord of my life, knowing that the sole purpose and fulfilment of my life is to have your glorious darshan, you have walked all the way and come along with Mother Janaki to bestow your grace and blessings upon me!"

Once, Tyagaraja went to witness a program by a touring group. The artists performed to a song in raga Ananda Bhairavi: "Mathura nagarilo", where the Gopis are asking Krishna, who had blocked their path, to give them way so that they could go to Mathura to sell milk. Tyagaraja was overjoyed at the beautiful performance of the artists. He immensely praised and wholeheartedly blessed them. They were overwhelmed to receive such appreciation from the great Musician-Saint. The head of the troupe offered his salutations and made a strange and unique request. He asked for Ananda Bhairavi Raga as a gift from Tyagaraja! Everyone including Tyagaraja was surprised. Tyagaraja asked him for the reason. He said, "In the years to come, people will hear and read of your greatness as a devotee of Lord Rama and a Musician-

Composer par excellence. People will also read and hear about this event where you gave away Ananda Bhairavi Raga as a gift to a small and insignificant musical troupe like ours. Along with your immortal glories, we will also be remembered and become immortal! Our lives will become blessed and fulfilled!!" Tyagaraja was stunned at his sweet innocence, and promised them that in future he would not compose any kirtan in this raga. Hence, only three kirtans written by Tyagaraja in Raga Ananda Bhairavi prior to this event are available.

Tyagaraja continued to teach music to anyone who wanted to learn from him. He composed around 24,000 kirtans, but only around 700 are available. His kritis are simple, but full of devotion. They contain the essence of the scriptures. Tyagaraja chose music as his path to God realization: NAADOPAASANA. His Pancharatna Kritis are well known and every year during Sri Tyagaraja Aradhana, these kritis are sung by musicians who gather there to offer their sangeeta seva.

When Tyagaraja knew that his time to leave his physical body was approaching, he took the vow of sanyasa. Lord Rama appeared in his dream, and told him that he would be bestowed with mukti or liberation after ten days, which Tyagaraja has recorded in one of his kirtans. On the sacred Pushya bahula panchami day, Tyagaraja Swami attained samadhi and merged with Lord Sri Rama to become one with Him.

"SRI RAMA! JAYA RAMA! JAYA JAYA RAMA!"

12. Hanuman removes the Sankat of Lord Shani!

Ravana, the King of Lanka was an erudite scholar, an accomplished musician, and a great astrologer. He waged a war on the devatas and defeated them. He captured all the nine planets (Nava Grahas) and brought them with him to Lanka. He exhibited his strength, might, and power by making the planets lie down face downwards, and used them as steps to ascend his throne daily. When his son, Meghanatha, was about to be born, Ravana decided to put all the nine planets in their favourable houses and positions so that his son would become powerful and invincible. The devatas got worried and sought the help of Sage Narada.

Sage Narada went to Ravana's assembly at their request. He saw all the planets lying face-down and being used as steps to the throne. Narada envisaged a plan. He glorified Ravana and told him that he should not be walking on the back of the planets, but should step and walk on their chest! That would prove to the Gods, Navagrahas, and everyone else how mighty and powerful the King of Lanka was! Ravana got carried away by Narada's words and turned all the planets around, face upwards, so that he could walk on their chest. As Ravana happily stepped and walked over them, Lord Shani's (Saturn) gaze fell upon him. It is well known that if Shani's gaze falls on anyone, it results in endless trouble and misfortunes. Shani's gaze had now fallen on Ravana! His troubles were about to start!!

Narada, after having accomplished the purpose of his visit, walked away happily. However, Ravana saw through the plan of the devatas. He was furious. He tied up Shani and confined him in a remote and dark room where nobody could find him. Shani, who gives trouble (sankat) to everyone with a mere glance, was confined and kept in the dark. He himself was now in 'sankat!'

Years passed by. When Hanuman was searching for Seeta in Ravana's palace, he heard a noise from one of the rooms. He opened the room and went inside. Hanuman found Shani tied up there. He quickly untied Shani and set him free. Lord Shani was happy that he had been freed, but Shani's gaze had fallen on Hanuman! It meant trouble and difficulties for Hanuman because of Shani! The Laws of Nature are very strict and no one can escape from them. When Lord Shani apprised him of the situation, Hanuman asked him to wait till he met Seeta, went back, and gave the news to Lord Rama. Shani waited....

Hanuman found Seeta in the Ashokavana, went back, and

gave the news to Rama. Rama, Lakshmana, Sugreeva, and the whole army of vanaras reached the tip of Bharat. They started building a bridge with rocks and trees to cross the ocean. Shani approached Hanuman when he was building the bridge with the other vanaras and decided to trouble him and put him through difficult situations. When Shani approached Hanuman, he said he was very busy and if Shani wanted to trouble him he could sit on his head. Shani comfortably sat on Hanuman's head. Hanuman ignored Lord Shani and continued helping the Vanaras to build the bridge. He lifted huge rocks and boulders and carried them on his head. Shani, who was sitting on Hanuman's head, started feeling the weight and burden of the rocks. He was unable to bear the pain caused by the heavy rocks and got off Hanuman's head. He realized that no one could trouble Hanuman because he was always chanting the Lord's name, and was always engaged in the service of the Lord.

Lord Shani was extremely pleased with Hanuman's devotion and service to Lord Rama. Hanuman had removed the 'sankat' of Shani who creates 'sankat' for everyone else! Lord Shani proclaimed that Hanuman would be known as SANKAT MOCHAN HANUMAN - the Lord who removes (Mochan) our troubles and difficulties (Sankat). Lord Shani further declared that whoever worships Hanuman on Shanivara (Saturday), the day dedicated to Shanidev, he would be able to overcome the adverse effects of Shani Bhagavan.

13. Nandi moves for Nandanar's sake!

Nandanar was a great devotee of Lord Shiva. He is one of the 63 Shaivite Saints who are known as Nayanars. Nandanar belonged to a small village known as Adhanur in Tamil Nadu. He belonged to a community that made percussion instruments. In those days, the upper caste community looked down on the members of Nandanar's community. After his daily work, Nandanar would spend most of his time singing the glories of the Lord.

Nandanar once visited Lord Shiva's temple at Thiruppunkoor. Since he was not allowed to enter the temple, he stood outside and prayed fervently to the Lord. He longed to have darshan of the

Lord from far, but the huge Nandi was right in front of the Lord. It was obstructing his view. Nandanar prayed to Nandi to move a little so that he could have a glimpse of the Lord. His prayers were answered and Nandi moved a little so that Nandanar could have darshan of Lord Shiva! Even to this day, Nandi is tilted slightly to one side in this temple!

Nandanar cherished a deep desire to go to Chidambaram and have darshan of Lord Nataraja. Every day, people would ask him when he planned to visit Chidambaram. But the thought of not being allowed to enter the temple made him postpone his visit. Whenever someone asked Nandanar when he would visit the temple, he would tell people that he would go the next day. Every day he would tell people, "I will go tomorrow". All the people started mocking him. They concluded that he would never go to Chidambaram and started calling him "tirunalaipoovar", which means "one who will go tomorrow!"

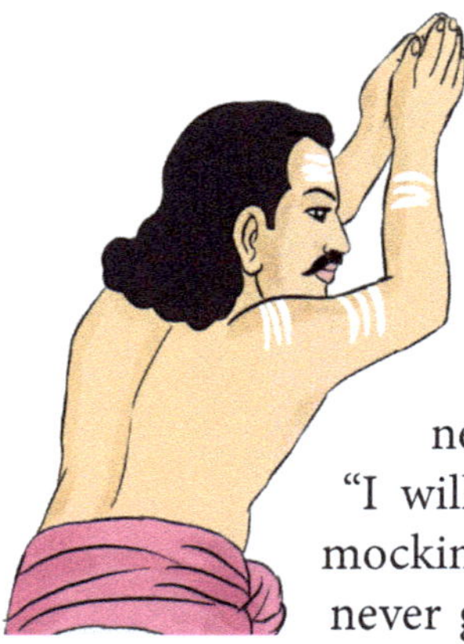

One fine day, Nandanar made up his mind and asked his landlord for permission to go to Chidambaram. The landlord told Nandanar that he would first have to plough his agricultural land and only then would he get permission. It was a huge task that would take days. Nandanar prayed to the Lord and started ploughing the field. He worked until late in the night. He was very exhausted and fell asleep. When he woke up the next morning, he saw that the entire field had been ploughed and was ready for sowing. The landlord was surprised and realized the greatness of Nandanar and immediately allowed him to go to Chidambaram.

Overwhelmed by the Lord's grace, Nandanar happily proceeded to Chidambaram, but he was not allowed to enter the temple. Singing the glories of Lord Sankara, he went round the holy city a number of times. Lord Shiva decided that it was time the world realized the greatness of Nandanar and his supreme devotion. The Lord appeared in Nandanar's dream and beckoned him to enter the temple. The next day, in the morning, Nandanar joyously started walking towards the temple. When he reached the temple, he saw that the purohits had lit up a huge Vedic fire for a yagna. His mind soaked in single-pointed devotion for the Lord, oblivious of his surroundings, Nandanar walked straight into the fire-kund that was right in front of him. Everyone was stunned at the sight of Nandanar entering the homa-kund. But nothing happened to him! He came out of the fire unscathed. Nandanar's physical form was shining like burnished gold! The presence of an inexplicable divine aura around him was evident. The priests realized the greatness of the Lord's devotee and respectfully escorted him into the sanctum of the Lord. In the presence of all those assembled, Nandanar merged and disappeared to become one with Parameshwara: the Lord-of-his-heart!

14. Ravana seeks help from Bali Chakravarti to fight Rama

Lord Rama, along with his vanara army crossed the ocean and reached Lanka to fight with Ravana and rescue Seeta who was in his captivity. What followed was a fierce battle between the armies of Sri Rama and Ravana. Every day, Ravana's army suffered defeat. He lost many of his prominent and mighty warriors. Extremely worried, Ravana decided to seek help from Bali Chakravarti - the grandson of Prahlada who was ruling over Sutala-loka (lower or nether world).

Ravana reached Sutala-loka. When he tried to enter Bali's kingdom, he was stopped by the guard at the entrance. Whenever he tried to enter, he was again stopped by the mighty and powerful guard who was protecting Bali's kingdom. The guard was none other than Lord Vamana himself. Unable to overpower Vamana, Ravana became invisible and tried to enter the kingdom again, but nothing was invisible to the Lord and he stopped Ravana.

Ravana reduced his form to the size of a small insect and quickly tried to enter, but Vamana stopped him and placed his foot on Ravana. Unable to bear the pain of the Lord's feet on him, Ravana lay there gasping for breath. The Lord could have crushed him, but he did not. Ravana was destined to be killed by Lord Rama. Since Ravana came in contact with the Lord's lotus feet, his body became pure enough to receive Lord Rama's divine arrow! Finally, Vamana released Ravana, and allowed him to enter the kingdom of Bali.

Ravana met Bali and requested him to help him in his fight with Lord Rama. Bali was aware of everything that had happened in Lanka. He also knew that it was the Lord who had been born as Rama to kill Ravana. Ravana had come requesting for help, and it was the duty of a King (Bali) to help all those who sought his help. Bali told the King of Lanka that he would help him on one condition. He took Ravana to an open land where there was a perfectly circular, huge mountainous golden object studded with diamonds and other precious gems.

Bali gifted the priceless object to Ravana. He told him that if he could lift it and take it with him, then he would consider helping him. Ravana could not lift the heavy object. He tried again with all his twenty hands and all his might, but the huge object did not move even an inch. Bali then asked Ravana to step back and look at it again. Wonder of wonders! The huge mountainous object looked like an ear-ring. It was one of the earrings of Hiranyakashipu who had been killed by Lord Narasimha. During the fight between the Lord and the Rakshasa, his ear-ring had fallen down to the nether world. Ravana had been Hiranyakashipu in his previous birth, but he could not even lift the ear-ring that he used to wear in his previous birth! Bali questioned Ravana's might and strength and advised him to give up his vanity

and arrogance. Bali forewarned Ravana that it was Lord Vishnu himself who had come down as Lord Rama to defeat and kill him. The purpose of the Lord's avatar would not be in vain.

Bali Chakravarti's timely advice did not go down well with Ravana. He returned to Lanka and engaged in a fierce battle with Lord Rama. Ultimately, Ravana was killed by Sri Rama and his noble and pious brother Vibhishana was crowned as the King of Lanka.

15. Sri Krishna and Paal-payasam!

Lord Krishna is worshipped as Parthasarathi, the charioteer of Arjuna at Ambalappuzha in the Alappuzha district of Kerala. The Lord has a whip in one hand and conch in the other. The temple was built by the local ruler during the 17th century. The unique feature of this temple is the PAAL-PAYASAM (rice and milk kheer) that is offered to the Lord as naivedya and distributed as prasad to all the devotees. According to local legends, Lord Guruvayoorappan comes to receive the Paal-payasam daily!

Chembakassery Pooradam Thirunal Deva-Narayana Thampuran was the king of this region. He was a great devotee of

Lord Krishna. He was very good at the game of dice (chathurangam). One day, Sri Krishna disguised as a sadhu approached the king and challenged him for a game of dice. The king, who was an expert in the dice-game, readily agreed. Now, there has to be a prize for the winner of the game. The king was confident that he would win the game. He asked the sadhu what he wanted in case he happened to win the game. The Lord told the king that he did not have any big demands since he was a sadhu who led a simple life. He only wanted a few grains of rice as measured by the number of squares on the dice-game board. One grain of rice for the first square, two grains for the second square, four grains for the third square, eight grains for the fourth square, sixteen grains for the fifth etc., by the process of doubling (exponential growth!). The king readily agreed.

The king confidently participated in the dice-game with the Lord, but he lost the game. According to the terms and conditions of the game, the king asked for rice to be brought so that he could give it to the sadhu as promised. He started calculating and placing the grains of rice in each square. Suddenly, he realized that this was a measurement on a very large scale! A sixty-four square dice-game board needs trillions of tons of rice!! All the rice from the granary was brought and it was still short of the required amount!

The king was in a dilemma because he was unable to fulfil the requirements of the sadhu. This was unpardonable. He knew that this was no ordinary sadhu. He prayed to the sadhu to help him with a solution. Lord Krishna revealed his true form to the king. The king was overwhelmed on having had the unique and good fortune of playing the dice-game with none other than the Lord himself. Indeed, what a blessing! Since the king was unable to fulfil the conditions that had been put forth prior to the game, the Lord told the king to serve "PAAL-PAYASAM" to the pilgrims daily until the debt was cleared. The king joyously agreed and started the unique tradition of offering PAAL-PAYASAM as Naivedya to Sri Krishna daily.

Every day, early in the morning, the preparation of large quantities of paal-payasam begins. Those in-charge of preparing the payasam seek the Lord's permission at every stage of adding ingredients into the huge cooking vessel. When the sugar is being added to the payasam, one of them comes to the door and loudly calls out - "VAASUDEVA!" This is to inform the Lord to come for naivedya since the payasam is almost ready! Generally, a small portion of the food is offered as naivedya at the Lord's altar. However, in this temple, the entire quantity of Paal-payasam prepared is offered to the Lord. The payasam filled vessels are carried to the altar to the accompaniment of shankha-naada. The paal-payasam is then offered to Sri Krishna and then served to all the devotees who come to the temple. The paal-payasam has immense medicinal value and benefits and hence, it is known as GOPALA KASHAYAM.

"May Sri Krishna, the Madhuradipathi (the Lord of Bliss), the Lover of PAAL-PAYASAM, reside in our minds and render it pure and sattvic (like milk), fill it with sweet devotion (like sugar) and finally grant the State of Realisation unto us. The PAYASAM represents the State of Realisation."

"Sri Krishna Govinda Hare Murare! Hey Natha Narayana Vaasudeva!!"

16. Origin of Lalitha Sahasranama

Surya (Sun) and Aruna (Dawn) were Sage Kashyapa's sons. Surya was beautiful and radiant whereas Aruna was deformed. However, Aruna was a great devotee of Lord Shiva. Pleased with his devotion, the Lord made him Surya's charioteer. He proclaimed that the time just before sunrise would be known as Arunodaya.

Surya always looked down on Aruna and humiliated him because his body was deformed. When Lord Shiva came to know about this, he was very angry and withdrew Surya's lustre and brilliance. As a consequence, Surya became dark. He realized his mistake and pleaded with the Lord. The Lord told him to undergo severe penance to regain his lustre. Lord Sun came to the sacred kshetra called Thirumeeyachur (Tamil Nadu) and worshipped Lord Shiva. When he did not get his golden lustre back even after months of austerity, he cried out loudly to the Lord. His loud and thunderous voice disturbed the serenity of the place. Parvati, who was there along with the Lord, became very angry and was about to pronounce a curse on Lord Sun.

Sankara immediately intervened and told her that Lord Sun was already under a curse and another curse would be devastating for him. Shiva told Parvati to calm down and invoked the "shanta" (peace) aspect in her. She immediately became calm. The Lord gave her the name SHANTA NAYAKI. She also became known as SRI LALITHAMBIKA. From Shanta Nayaki's mouth, the presiding deities of speech, the 'Vak-Devis' manifested and glorified her through a thousand beautiful names. These thousand names came to be known as LALITHA SAHASRANAMA. Lord Sun was relieved of his curse and with the Lord's grace, he regained his lost golden lustre. Since the Lord had removed the cloud of darkness covering the Sun, Shiva became known as 'Sri Meghanatha'. During the month of Chithirai, the sun's rays fall directly on Lord Meghanatha for seven days. This is considered Surya's devotional offering to Lord Shiva.

Sri Lalithambika, also known as Sundara Nayaki sits on the throne known as 'Srichakraraja' as the Empress (Maharani) with her right leg folded and placed on the left. The Lalitha Sahasranama, which was given out by Vak-Devis, was first revealed to Lord Hayagriva, an incarnation of Lord Vishnu who is also the presiding deity of knowledge and intelligence. Subsequently, Lord Hayagriva taught the Lalitha Sahasranama to his disciple, Sage Agastya, and asked him to worship Sri Lalithambika at Thirumeeyachur. Sage Agastya went to this sacred place and invoked Sri Lalithambika by chanting the Lalitha

Sahasranama. The divine Mother was pleased and appeared in front of him as 'Navaratnas – the nine gems'. Overwhelmed at this rare and unique darshan, Sage Agastya composed and sang the 'Lalitha Navaratna Mala'. From Sri Lalithambika to Hayagriva, and then through Sage Agastya the sacred Lalitha Sahasranama reached the mortal human beings. Even to this day, those who want to learn and chant the Lalitha Sahasranama undertake a pilgrimage to this sacred place to seek Devi's blessings.

This sacred place is so peaceful that even Sri Durga who stands on mahishasura, is 'shanta-swaroopini' with a parrot in her hand! It is believed that the parrot carries the messages and pleas of the devotees to Lalithambika. Even to this day, in the evening, parrots can be seen flying from the temple of Durga towards the temple of Lalithambika! Another unique feature of this temple is that Goddess Lalithambika wears a pair of anklets that go completely around the feet of the idol. There is a narrow opening at the ankles of the deity just sufficient for the chain of the anklets to go through! Devotees who come to the temple bring anklets with them as their devout offering to Devi.

On the auspicious VIJAYADASAMI day, plantain leaves are spread over an area of 15ft in length and 5ft in width in the sanctum. It is divided into three sections. In the first section closest to the deity, 100 kg of sweet pongal is spread. In the next section, 100kg of tamarind rice and in the third section 100 kg of curd rice is spread – all one after the other. In the middle of the sweet pongal, a huge hollow or trough is created and a large amount of liquid ghee is poured. It is known as the GHEE WELL. After the special alankara of Sri Lalithambika, the curtains of the sanctum are drawn apart and arati is performed. The reflection of Sri Lalithambika can be seen in the 'ghee well!' This unique, beautiful, and awesome darshan is considered extremely auspicious. Devotees throng the shrine in large numbers on Vijayadasami day to have a glimpse of Sri Lalithambika in the GHEE WELL!

The 'ghee-well' represents a pure and sattvic mind. The sweet pongal around the 'ghee-well' represents the layers of matter of the individual personality. The reflection of Sri Lalithambika (Paramatma or Parabrahma) in the 'ghee-well' (mind) represents the 'Vision of the Divine' which is the State of Enlightenment or Mukti. This is the real and everlasting Victory or Fulfillment (Vijaya)!

17. The Supremacy of Devotion

Lord Krishna accompanied by his consort, Satyabhama, went to the kingdom of Pragjyotispura on Garuda. He killed the rakshasa, Narakasura, with his powerful Sudarshana Chakra. The mighty Garuda helped the Lord in the battle by destroying Narakasura's army with its beak, wings, and claws. Satyabhama, who was adept in warfare, helped the Lord in the battle.

When the Lord returned to Dwaraka, he found Satyabhama, Garuda, and Sudarshana Chakra full of pride and vanity. Satyabhama was proud of her beauty, wealth, and skills in warfare. She always looked down on Rukmini who was none other than Goddess Lakshmi herself. She also spoke very lightly about Seeta, the Lord's consort in his Rama avatar. Garuda was proud of his enormous strength and swift speed. Not only was he instrumental in carrying the Lord, but he had also helped the Lord destroy Narakasura's army. Sudarshana Chakra was arrogant of its lightning speed and whirling precision in striking and destroying the Lord's enemies. The Lord envisaged a plan to destroy the ego of all the three.

Lord Krishna summoned Hanuman, his best and most humble devotee to Dwaraka and narrated everything to him. As per the Lord's divine plan, Hanuman reached the palace garden and started uprooting the trees, breaking the branches, and eating the fruits. The guards tried to prevent him, but could not. They ran to Sri Krishna and reported the matter to him. Sri Krishna called Garuda and asked him to go with the army and capture the monkey that was destroying the garden. Garuda, filled with vanity, told the Lord that there was no need for the army. He would capture the monkey single-handed and bring him to the Lord. Sri Krishna agreed and Garuda swiftly went to the garden. He introduced himself as the king of birds. He spoke about his might and glory and ordered Hanuman to stop destroying the garden, and come along with him to the palace to meet Sri Krishna. Hanuman refused and told Garuda that he would not meet anyone, other than his Lord, Sri Rama. Both of them argued and Garuda was ready to fight with Hanuman. Not wanting to hurt him, Hanuman gently pushed Garuda, but that was enough to toss Garuda into the ocean! Garuda came out of the ocean, dripping with water, and went to Sri Krishna. He narrated everything to the Lord. Sri Krishna told him to go back and tell Hanuman that Lord Rama wanted to see him. Garuda went back to the garden. He stood at the edge of the garden, far from Hanuman's reach, and conveyed the Lord's message to him. Hanuman immediately agreed to meet the Lord. Garuda offered to carry Hanuman to the

Lord's presence quickly, but Hanuman declined the offer saying it would delay him. Garuda wondered how Hanuman could reach the Lord's presence quickly without his help. He went back swiftly and was astonished to see Hanuman already present near the entrance of the palace. Hanuman had reached there before Garuda. Totally humbled, Garuda realized that he was no match for Hanuman in respect of strength or speed. He prostrated to the Lord and begged for forgiveness.

In the meantime, the Lord manifested himself as Lord Rama and asked Satyabhama to accompany him as Seeta. He summoned Sudarshana Chakra and told him not to allow anyone into the palace. With tremendous speed, the dazzling Sudarshana Chakra started whirling and circling round the palace to keep guard.

In all eagerness to meet Lord Rama, Hanuman rushed towards the palace, but Sudarshana stopped him and refused entry to him. Hanuman was annoyed at the obstacle in front of him. He was unwilling to engage himself in another encounter, so he quickly grabbed the Sudarshana Chakra and put it in his mouth! He made his way into the inner chambers of the palace. He was overwhelmed with joy to meet Lord Rama. He ran to the Lord and prostrated to him. He released the Sudarshana Chakra from his mouth and told the Lord that he had swallowed the divine disc only because it had prevented his entry into the palace. Sudarshana Chakra, which was almost suffocated in Hanuman's throat, was relieved. Sudarshana too realized Hanuman's strength and might. The Lord's Chakra prostrated to both of them and retired.

Hanuman started looking around. Lord Rama asked him what was the matter. He said he was looking around for his Mother, Devi Seeta. Hanuman saw Satyabhama in Seeta's attire, but he knew very well that she was not Lord Rama's divine consort. He even asked the Lord who the unknown woman standing next to him was. Satyabhama was extremely embarrassed. She realized that nobody could be a substitute for Seeta's simplicity, devotion, humility, grace and poise. Satyabhama's beauty, wealth, and skills were no match for Rukmini who was Seeta in the previous incarnation.

All three of them - Garuda, Sudarshana Chakra, and Satyabhama realized that the Lord appreciates and responds only to single-pointed devotion and total surrender.

18. Raga Sankarabharana Mortgaged!

The Maratha Kings who ruled over Thanjavur (Tamil Nadu) were great patrons of art. They patronised, encouraged, and honoured great stalwarts of Carnatic Music and therefore, Thanjavur became a prominent centre of Carnatic Music. Narasayyar was a prominent and well known court musician of the then ruler Serfoji. On one occasion, Narasayya elaborated and sang the Raga Sankarabharana for hours in the presence of the king. The king was extremely happy with Narasayyar's mastery over the raga and declared that he would be known as SANKARABHARANA NARASAYYAR in future.

Once, Narasayyar was in dire need of money due to a financial crisis. He did not know whom to approach, and he was hesitant to ask anyone for help. But when it became inevitable, he went to meet Ramabhadra Moopanar who was a wealthy landlord and a great lover of music. Ramabhadra Moopanar lived in Kapisthalam near Thanjavur. He was very happy to see Narasayyar. He received him, offered his hospitality, and asked him to stay in his house for a few days. After a couple of days, Narasayyar asked Moopanar for a loan very hesitatingly. The generous Moopanar was shocked. He would have willingly given Narasayyar, whom he adored, whatever amount he wanted. And here the great musician was asking for a loan. This was a sensitive issue. Taking care not to hurt Narasayyar's feelings, he asked him how much he wanted. Narasayyar told Moopanar that he wanted eighty gold coins (sovereigns). Moopanar agreed to give the eighty gold coins as a loan and asked Narasayya if he had brought anything to pledge, say, an 'abharana' (gold jewellry), as security.

Narasayyar told him that he had a unique and special 'abharana' to pledge with him, which could not be seen but only heard! Moopanar was surprised and asked for the 'abharana'. Narasayyar told him that he had the rare 'abharana' called SANKARA-ABHARANA Raga, which he was ready to pledge in return for the gold coins. Moopanar was stunned and surprised, but restraining himself and his feelings, he formally went through the normal procedure of documenting the transaction. Eighty gold coins were given to Narasayyar as a loan, and he pledged his favourite Raga Sankarabharana as security to the money lender. The condition was that Narasayyar would not sing Raga Sankarabharana until he cleared the debt. Narasayyar collected the gold coins and left for Thanjavur. From that day onwards, he refrained from singing the Sankarabharana Raga in all his subsequent concerts. Music-lovers missed Narasayyar's Sankarabharana Raga, but nobody knew the reason.

At the time, Appu Rayar was serving as the Dewan of Thanjavur and Tiruchirapalli under the East India Company. There was a marriage function in his family in the town of Kumbhakonam. He wanted to celebrate the wedding on a grand scale and decided to arrange music concerts by eminent artists during the marriage function. Narasayyar was also one amongst the performers. Large number of people gathered on the day of Narasayyar's concert. Since Narasayyar was known for his rendering of Raga Sankarabharana, Appu Rayar requested him to start the program with Raga Sankarabharana. Narasayyar politely declined to sing the Sankarabharana. After much insistence, Narasayyar told Appu Rayar the reason. Appu Rayar was stunned. A RAGA mortgaged for a loan – he had never heard of it before. He immediately sent a messenger with a bag of eighty gold coins and the interest to Moopanar's place and asked him to bring back the promissory note.

After speaking with the messenger, Ramabhadra Moopanar realized the seriousness of the situation. He himself accompanied the messenger with the signed deed to Kumbhakonam. He apologized for having agreed to the mortgage of Sankarabharana Raga. He explained to Appu Rayar why he had handled the sensitive loan transaction issue with so much formality. He declined to take back the gold coins and asked Appu Rayar to give the gold coins, along with all the accrued interest, to Narasayyar. Moopanar also released the Sankarabharana Raga and requested Narasayyar to sing his favourite Sankarabharana Raga. All those assembled were astonished at the sequence of events that unfolded in front of them: A musician mortgaging a RAGA for a loan! An ardent music-lover ready to repay the loan with interest and another equally ardent music-lover declining to take back the amount he had given as a loan!! Nevertheless, everyone enjoyed the day's concert with Narasayyar at his best while rendering the Sankarabharana Raga!!!

19. Lord Nataraja's Ananda Tandava at Chidambaram

The Rishis who lived in Darukavana (pine forest) engaged themselves in intense tapas and yagnas continuously. Due to their meritorious activities, they became very powerful and consequently very arrogant and full of pride. They thought that they could control all the devatas because of their austerities and mantras-siddhis. When Lord Shiva heard of their attitude, he set out to destroy their pride. He disguised himself as a pious man. On the behest of Shiva, Lord Vishnu took the form of Mohini and accompanied Shiva as his wife. Both of them came to Darukavana. The rishis and their wives were totally mesmerized by the beauty and charm of the divine couple and became distracted from their austerities. A little later, the rishis realized that they had been distracted from their austerities and became angry.

The rishis started a yagna to attack and counter the couple without knowing that it was Lord Shiva and Vishnu in front of them. In the 'yagna-fire', they invoked a ferocious tiger and directed it towards Lord Shiva. The Lord killed the tiger and wore its skin around his waist. Next came a serpent from the sacrificial fire. Shiva seized it in his hand and wore it round his neck as an ornament. A wild elephant was invoked next, which the Lord easily killed. A demon called Apasmara (representing ignorance) was sent next. The Lord put him under his feet and rendered him immobile. Various hurdles and obstacles in the form of mantras were sent towards Lord Shiva. He converted them all into anklets and wore them round his feet. Having met all the challenges successfully, the Lord started his wonderful and most awesome cosmic dance called "Ananda Tandava" (the dance of eternal bliss). The Lord danced and Lord Vishnu watched the beautiful Tandava! The rishis were stunned at the breath-taking, beautiful Cosmic Nritya (Dance). Lord Shiva's Tandava represents Creation, Sustenance, and Dissolution. The rishis realized their mistake and prostrated to the Lord and asked for forgiveness.

After reaching Vaikunta, Lord Vishnu who was witness to the great Shiva Tandava narrated the entire episode and described the Tandava in particular to Adi Sesha. Adi Sesha was very eager to see the unique and divine dance of the Lord. Sri Hari told him to proceed to the Thillai forest (mangrove forest), which is Chidambaram (Tamil Nadu), and perform tapas. Adi Sesha manifested as Sage Patanjali and came to the Thillai forest. He was joined by Sage Vyaghrapada. They made a Shiva-linga and invoked and worshipped Lord Shiva in it.

Lord Shiva was pleased and performed the Tandava for them. Chidambaram was the only place in the universe that had the strength and stability to become the divine stage for the Lord of Dance, Nataraja for his Cosmic Dance. All the devatas, rishis, and gandharvas came to witness the dance. Celestial musicians sang. Narada played his veena and Nandi played the mridangam. The Vedas became the Lord's anklets! The devatas and rishis who had witnessed the great performance requested the Lord to continue his Nritya for the welfare of the whole world. Lord Nataraja agreed and made Chidambaram his abode.

Chidambaram means "covered or clothed with knowledge". The Lord is worshipped there in the form of Nataraja (with form), as crystal Linga (form-less), and as Akasha or Space-linga (invisible). Hence, this kshetra is one of the Pancha Mahabhuta Kshetras. There are five sabhas in which Lord Shiva performed five different types of Tandavas. Chidambaram is the Golden Sabha where the Lord performed the Ananda Tandava. The temple was designed and consecrated by Sage Patanjali himself who is the author of the 'Yoga Sutras'. Hence, the structure of the Chidambaram temple is similar to the entire structure of a human being. The temple is located at the centre point of the world's magnetic equator.

20. Raksha Bandhan

Raksha Bandhan is a day on which sisters tie the sacred thread (rakhi) on the wrist of their brothers. A sense of responsibility, well-being, bonding between family members, sharing, etc., is inculcated into the family members through the ritual of raksha-bandhan. The ritual signifies not only prayers for protection, health and long life for the brother, but also represents the brother's commitment to protect the dignity and honour of the sister.

However, in its larger perspective, Rakhi is known as RAKSHA SUTRA. The raksha-thread is first placed at the altar of the Lord. It is then tied round the wrist of the person (need not necessarily be the brother) invoking the Lord's grace and blessings for protection from all dangers, harms, calamities etc. Normally after offering it to the Lord, either the priest or the eldest member of the family ties it round the wrist of the individual. The sacred thread is also tied round the wrist when an individual makes a sankalpa or undertakes a vow. In this case, it is called 'kankana'. The individual then becomes committed to his sankalpa or vow and when the sankalpa or vow is fulfilled, the 'kankana' is removed. The colour (red, yellow etc.) of the thread depends upon the sankalpa. Undertaking a sankalpa or vow demands discipline and earnest self-effort on the part of the individual.

Goddess Lakshmi and Bali Chakravarti: As Vamana, Lord Vishnu made Bali Chakravarthi the king of the lower (nether) world, and promised to remain there as his security guard. However, the devatas wanted the Lord to return to Vaikunta. All the devatas requested Goddess Lakshmi to help them. Lakshmi reached Bali Chakravarti's kingdom in the guise of an ordinary woman and sought protection and shelter from him stating that her husband had left her and she was all alone. Bali gave Goddess Lakshmi shelter in his kingdom. Pleased with his hospitality, Lakshmi tied a RAKSHA-SUTRA on Bali's wrist on the full-moon day of the month of Shravan seeking the Lord's blessings for him. Bali was very pleased and told her to ask him for whatever she wanted and he would grant it. Lakshmi asked Bali to relieve her husband from the security work he was doing. Bali was surprised and asked her who her husband was. Then, Goddess Lakshmi and Sri Hari appeared in their true form and gave darshan to Bali. An overwhelmed Bali prostrated to the divine couple. Lord Vishnu was relieved of his security work. However, the Lord promised king Bali that he would always protect him and his kingdom. The Lord also assured Bali that he would visit his kingdom every year. Sri Hari and his consort went back to Vaikunta. Hence, the tradition of women tying the 'raksha-sutra' not only to brothers but to all their near and dear ones, wishing them plentitude and prosperity, peace and happiness. In turn, they promise to protect the dignity and honour of their mothers, sisters, and daughters.

Lord Krishna and Draupadi: Yudhisthira, the eldest of the Pandavas and king of Indraprastha decided to perform the Rajasuya Yaga. According to the customs and rituals, 'agra-puja' had to be performed, wherein a respectful and revered person is identified, worshipped, and duly honoured. In the galaxy of eminent scholars and mighty warriors, Lord Krishna was chosen. When Yudhisthira escorted Lord Krishna to the 'seat of honour', the evil-minded Sishupala who hated Lord Krishna insulted and abused Krishna in the royal assembly. When he crossed all limits and continued to abuse the Lord, Krishna invoked his mighty and powerful Sudarshana Chakra. It came at tremendous speed, struck Sishupala down, and returned to Lord Krishna's finger with the same speed. Krishna's finger was injured. It started bleeding because of the sharp edges of the speeding chakra. Everyone ran around trying to find something to bandage his finger and arrest the bleeding. Draupadi, the wife of the Pandavas, was standing nearby. She immediately tore a part of the end of her saree and wrapped it around Lord Krishna's finger and wound it around his wrist to keep it in its place. The Lord was very pleased with her devotion and spontaneity and told her that he was indeed indebted to her for all his life. Considering her as his own sister, Lord Krishna told her that whenever and wherever she needed him, he would be there to protect her. This little act of tying a small piece of her garment round his finger would one day become 'akshaya' (endless or infinite). Later on, when the Pandavas lost everything to

the Kauravas during the game of dice, Duryodhana's brother, Dushasana, dragged Draupadi into the assembly and tried to disrobe her. She invoked Lord Krishna at the time and the Lord protected her from the humiliation – miraculously, the saree she was wearing became 'akshaya' and protected her. Raksha Bandhan also signifies the Lord protecting his sister, Draupadi.

"The Lord, the Ultimate Cause of the whole Universe, Lord of Venkatadri is the Sole Protector and Saviour of my Life (Jeeva-Raksha)" ~ Sri Annamacharya (Musician-Saint).

21. Padmapada - Adi Sankara's disciple

Sanandana was a very bright and intelligent boy from the southern part of Bharat. After he finished his initial studies in his hometown, he decided to lead the life of a brahmachari. He travelled all the way to Kashi to meet a Guru under whose guidance he could progress further in his spiritual pursuits. At the time, Adi Sankara was in Kashi giving discourses on Advaita Philosophy.

When Sanandana met Adi Sankara, he was drawn towards

the Acharya. Sanandana knew that he had found his Guru. He offered his respectful prostrations and asked the Acharya to accept him as his disciple and initiate him into sanyasa. Seeing the keenness of the youngster, the Master agreed and took him as his disciple. Sanandana became Sankara's first disciple. Sanandana stayed with his Guru, serving and learning from him. Sanandana was extremely brilliant and absorbed the knowledge three times faster than anyone else. Sankara was highly pleased and appreciated his disciple's intellectual abilities. However, the other students misunderstood and thought that the teacher was more favourable to Sanandana and became jealous. Sankara understood what was going on in their minds, and decided that it was time for them to see and recognise the greatness of Sanandana for themselves.

One day, Sanandana was busy washing clothes on the banks of river Ganga. Sankaracharya, who was on the opposite bank of the river along with his disciples, loudly called, "Sanandana!" The moment Sanandana heard his name being called by his Guru, he immediately started walking towards his Master. He was on one side of the river and Sankara was on the other side. The actual path was around the river and it would take some time for him to reach the other side. The only thought in his mind while he was walking was that his Guru had suddenly called him, and he needed to get there as quickly as possible. He just walked the quickest path. To everyone's surprise, they found Sanandana walking on the waters of the river! Generally, the strong water currents would have washed him away. But lo! The moment he stepped into the water, a full blown lotus sprang up to support his foot.

When he put the next step forward, another lotus appeared in the waters to support his foot. Sanandana had no idea that he was walking on water. In his anxiety to reach his Guru quickly, he was almost running on water with every step being supported by a lotus! The other disciples who were watching this miracle were dumbfounded. They understood that it was Sanandana's absolute faith and total devotion for his Guru that made it possible for him to walk on water!

Sanandana came and prostrated to his Guru. Sankara smiled at his disciple and acknowledged him. All the disciples realized their mistake as well as the greatness of Sanandana and his devotion for his Guru. When Sankara pointed out to him the river behind, Sanandana looked back. He then realised that he had literally walked on water. At every step, since a lotus (padma) had appeared below his foot (pada), Adi Sankara gave him the name PADMAPADA : "feet supported by lotus".

Padmapada was one amongst the four principal disciples of Adi Sankara. He was in charge of the Govardhan Math at Puri in the eastern part of Bharat.

22. Lord Krishna's Gurudakshina

Lord Krishna and Balarama were invited to Mathura for a Dhanur-yagna by the evil tyrant king, Kamsa. Kamsa planned to kill both the brothers during the yagna. However, all his plans failed. Finally, Lord Krishna killed the wicked Kamsa. The Devatas were delighted, the Gandharvas sang and Apsaras danced in sheer joy and rained down showers of flowers. The wise and old Ugrasena, Krishna's grandfather, was released from prison and reinstalled on the throne of Mathura. Vasudeva and Devaki were overwhelmed to see their children, Krishna and Balarama, after so many years of longing and hoping.

Vasudeva approached his family Guru, Gargacharya, and in accordance with the sastras, had the Upanayana performed for both his children. Balarama and Krishna were initiated into the Gayatri-mantra. They were ready to commence the study of the Vedas. Gargacharya was well aware of the divinity of Krishna and Balarama. He spoke to Vasudeva and told him to send his sons to Guru Sandeepani, one of the greatest and foremost amongst the Acharyas who resided in Ujjain. Vasudeva agreed, and both Krishna and Balarama proceeded to Ujjain from Mathura.

Krishna and Balarama reached the ashram of Guru Sandeepani, offered their prostrations and introduced themselves to him. They prayed that they be accepted as his disciples. Seeing the unearthly divine glow on the smiling faces of Krishna and Balarama, Guru Sandeepani readily and whole-heartedly accepted them as his disciples. Krishna and Balarama reverentially and respectfully served their teacher with devotion. The best of the Acharyas, Guru Sandeepani, taught them the four Vedas and their six branches, the Upanishads, the Science of Archery along with the Mantras, Dharmasastras, Nyaya, Rajaneeti and other branches of knowledge. They mastered all the sixty four Arts in just sixty four days.

After completing their studies at the Gurukula, before leaving, Balarama and Krishna asked their Guru what they could offer as their Guru Dakshina. Guru Sandeepani was aware of the divinity of both his students. He was more than happy and fulfilled to have had them as his disciples. The Lord had chosen him as his teacher! What more could anyone desire? However, Sandeepani's wife urged him to ask Krishna to bring back their only son, whom they had lost in the ocean at Prabhasa Kshetra, back to life. Krishna promised to bring back the child. Krishna and Balarama

went to Prabhasa. Krishna summoned the presiding deity of the ocean and asked for Sandeepani's son who had been swallowed up by the waves.

The Lord of the Ocean told Krishna that he had not taken away the child. He further told the Lord that a rakshasa called Panchajana lived in the ocean. To conceal his identity from the devatas, he had been hiding in the deep waters inside a conch. When Sandeepani's son was playing on the shores of the ocean, the rakshasa had dragged the child into the waters.

The Lord immediately plunged into the waters, fought the rakshasa and killed him. The Lord took with him the conch which became known as Panchajanya. Krishna did not find his Guru's child in the ocean. Subsequently, Krishna and Balarama went to the city of Lord Death, which was known as Samyamani. Lord Krishna announced his arrival by blowing the Panchajanya. Lord Yama immediately came forward and offered his prostrations to both of them. He asked them with folded hands how he could serve the Lord. Krishna said, "Bring the son of my Guru Sandeepani whom you have carried away due to the child's destiny." Yama immediately brought the child and presented him to Krishna. The Lord took the child with him to his Guru's ashram. Sandeepani and his wife were overjoyed to get their son back.

Lord Krishna requested Sandeepany to ask for something else as Gurudakshina. However, Sandeepani who was more than fulfilled said, "O my child! Can any desire remain unfulfilled for a Guru who has you as his disciple. You both have paid your GURUDAKSHINA fully. Return to your home. May your divine glory purify all those who come in contact with you. May your knowledge ever remain fresh in your memory and be available to you whenever you need it."

Feeling extremely happy and totally fulfilled, Lord Krishna and Balarama offered their prayerful prostrations to Guru Sandeepani, and returned to Mathura with the blessings of their Guru.

23. Sri Rama Anjaneya Yuddha

Once, there was a debate in Kailasa whether Rama's incomparable strength and might was greater OR the power and glory of Rama Nama. Nobody could arrive at any conclusion. Sage Narada, who also happened to be there, envisaged a plan to solve the problem.

Narada took the help of Maya, who is none other than the Lord's sakti. As told by Narada, she created rakshasic creatures and sent them to the kingdom of Kashi, whose king was a great devotee of Lord Rama. The monstrous creatures started harassing and troubling all the people of Kashi. Seeing his people in trouble, the king set out to destroy the demonic forces. The terrible rakshasas started to flee from Kashi and the king pursued them. One of them assumed the form of a sadhu and entered Sage Vishwamitra's ashram. The king discharged an arrow, which hit the rakshasa disguised as a sadhu. Sage Vishwamitra became very angry when he saw an innocent resident of the ashram being targeted. However much the king tried to convince the sage that this was a rakshasic form, he would not listen to him. He walked away, warning the king that he would have to pay for his wrongdoings.

Sage Vishwamitra reached Ayodhya. He narrated what had happened in his ashram and asked Sri Rama to punish the wrongdoer with the penalty of death. Rama agreed. When the Lord heard that it was the king of Kashi who was his devotee, he was taken aback, but he had given his word to the Sage.The king, who was also unhappy at the turn of events, was going back to his kingdom when he met Sage Narada. On being questioned, he narrated everything to Narada. Narada asked him not to worry and sent him to Anjanadevi, Lord Hanuman's mother, for protection. Anjanadevi immediately assured the king of her protection. When Hanuman met his mother, Anjanadevi told him everything that had happened. To keep his mother's promise, he too readily granted his protection to the king. The king happily stayed with Hanuman. Neither the king nor Hanuman or his mother knew that Rama had given his word to Vishwamitra to punish the king.

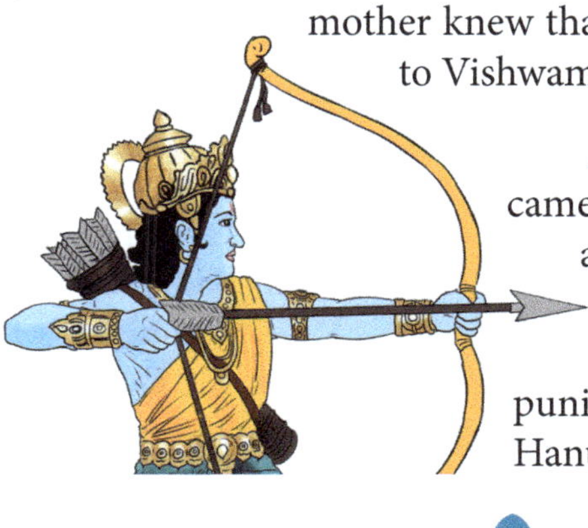

At this juncture, Narada came along and told Hanuman and his mother that it was Rama who had promised Sage Vishwamitra to punish the king with death. Hanuman was shocked and saddened by the turn of events. It meant that he had to encounter none other than Sri Rama, his dear Lord and Master. In Ayodhya, Rama also came to know that Hanuman had promised to protect the king. He was unhappy as well. Both Rama and Hanuman had given their word, and both of them were very firm about not breaking their promise. It meant a conflict between the two of them!

Lord Rama and Hanuman met. The Lord asked Hanuman to surrender the king to him. Hanuman refused to do so, saying that he had learnt to keep his word from Rama himself! Words were exchanged - in the beginning soft and gentle, but slowly they became harsh and strong.

Finally, Rama decided to use his strength and might against Hanuman. Hanuman was very clear. He would not fight the Lord; how could he? He asked the king to hide behind him and sat down facing the Lord. He closed his eyes and started chanting RAMA...RAMA... RAMA. Rama released arrow after arrow towards Hanuman very reluctantly. The arrows, which never ever turned back and surely and always hit the target, could not even touch Hanuman! In front of the power of Rama Nama, the strength and might of the arrows simply lost their power and paled into insignificance! All the devatas assembled in the sky to watch this unique encounter between RAMA-SHAKTI and RAMA-BHAKTI!

Finally, Rama decided to use the Brahmastra and bring Hanuman out of his samadhi. By then, everyone had understood the POWER and GLORY of RAMA NAMA. Narada narrated everything to Sage Vishwamitra and took him to the venue. Lord Brahma and Lord Shiva also arrived there. Vishwamitra told

Rama about the play of Maya-sakti to prove to the whole world the power, glory, and supremacy of the Lord's name: SRI RAMA. NOTHING can stand in comparison with and become equal to RAMA NAMA!

Hanuman woke up from his samadhi, prostrated to the Lord, and asked him for forgiveness for having stood against his own Lord to keep his mother's word. The king of Kashi was overjoyed to have the glorious darshan of the Lord-of-his-heart and he offered his prayerful prostrations to Sri Rama. Everyone went back to their divine destination. Sage Narada also went on his way supremely happy, singing the Lord's glories!

"Sri Rama! Jaya Rama! Jaya Jaya Rama!"

24. Devi Mookambika

Kola Maharshi resided in the valley of the Kodachadri hills near Udupi (Karnataka). He undertook intense tapas to propitiate Lord Shiva. Pleased with his tapas, Lord Shiva appeared before him and granted him a boon. The Sage said that he wanted nothing for himself. However, he prayed to the Lord to take up His abode in the sacred valley for the welfare of the people. The Lord agreed and manifested in the form of a Linga. The Sage wanted the presence of Devi Parvati, the Lord's divine consort, along with the Lord. To fulfil the request of the rishi, a golden line appeared on the Shiva linga to indicate the presence of Shakti along with Shiva. The place became known as Kollur.

There lived a rakshasa called Kaumasura who went about creating havoc amongst the pious and virtuous people. He performed tapas to seek the boon of becoming invincible and immortal from the Creator, Lord Brahma. Pleased with the rakshasa's tapas, Lord Brahma appeared before him. Kaumasura was about to ask for the boon of becoming invincible. His tapas had been fruitful and the Creator was about to bestow whatever boon he wanted on him. All the devatas were worried. If Brahma gave him the boon of becoming invincible, he would become a threat to all the three worlds. They all invoked Vagdevi, the Goddess of Speech, and asked her to withdraw her grace from him. She agreed and withdrew the power of speech from the rakshasa. As a result, he became dumb. He could not ask the Lord for anything. From that day onwards, he came to be known as Mookasura. Mooka means 'dumb'.

The angry Mookasura continued to trouble the devatas and sages. The devatas again prayed to Shakti. Devi appeared before them. All the devatas, including Brahma, Vishnu and Shiva along with their Sakti-s, Saraswathi, Lakshmi and Parvati, transferred their powers to Shakti. There was a fierce battle between Shakti and Mookasura and she finally killed Mookasura. From that day onwards she became known as Mookambika. She represents the power of speech (Vak) which destroys dumbness (mookatva).

Years later, Adi Sankara was travelling through this region. Pleased with his tapas, Vagdevi appeared in front of him desirous of bestowing a boon upon him. Sankara was overjoyed at the darshan of the Mother of the Universe and prayed to her to come with him and dwell in the land of his birth. She agreed to come with him, but she put forth one condition. She would follow him, but he should not turn back and look. Sankara agreed and started walking. Mookambika followed him. He could hear the sound of her anklets. As they were approaching Kollur, Sankara suddenly stopped hearing the sound of Devi's anklets. He turned around to check whether Devi was still following him. As per her condition, Mookambika or Vagdevi remained permanently in Kollur, on the banks of the sacred Sauparnika river.

Sri Mookambika is the Goddess who destroys mookatva

(ignorance) and confers speech (Knowledge) to all those who invoke her. Hence, Devi Mookambika is invoked on the most auspicious day of Vijayadasami during the Navaratri festival, and "Akshara Abhyasa" is performed for little children before they start their formal education.

25. Hanuman & the Bell

Lord Rama, along with his consort Seeta and brother Lakshmana, went to the forest for fourteen years to keep the promise his father had given to Kaikeyi. While they were living in the forest, Seeta was abducted by Ravana, the king of Lanka. Rama and Lakshmana reached Kishkindha during their search for Seeta. They were able to locate Seeta in Lanka with Hanuman's help. The huge vanara army under the leadership of Rama and Sugreeva was ready to proceed to Lanka. Rama assured the vanaras and their families that all the vanaras accompanying him would return safely. They built a bridge across the ocean and crossed over to the other side. The battle between Rama and Ravana was about to start. The Lord told Sugreeva to take count of the vanaras who had accompanied him.

There was a fierce battle between Sri Rama and Ravana. Finally, Lord Rama killed Ravana and his brother Kumbhakarna. Seeta was released from captivity and she joined her Lord. Ravana's brother, Vibhishana, who was Rama's devotee was crowned as the king of Lanka. Before leaving for Ayodhya, Rama asked Sugreeva, the Vanara king, to once again take count of the vanaras. They found a few vanaras missing. Rama called Hanuman and asked him to accompany him in search of the vanaras. Both Rama and Hanuman walked to the battlefield and carefully started searching for the missing vanaras - dead or alive.

When Ravana's brother, Kumbhakarna, had come to fight with Rama, he rode in a chariot that had a canopy decked with golden bells. Since Kumbhakarna had a huge personality, his chariot, its canopy, and the bells were also proportionately huge. During the battle, an arrow from Rama's side struck one of the huge bells and it fell down. A few vanaras, short in stature, known as 'dwarf vanaras', got trapped under the huge bell. They called out for help but nobody heard them. It was completely dark inside. A tiny hole near the ring of the bell kept them from suffocating. An old monkey who was with them told them not to lose hope and chant the sacred name of Lord Rama. He whose mere name kept afloat huge rocks and prevented them from sinking would surely save them from the grip of death. All the monkeys closed their eyes and fervently started chanting, "Sri Rama...Sri Rama... Sri Rama".

When Rama, Hanuman, and the others were walking in the battlefield looking for the vanaras, Rama noticed the huge bell and stopped in front of it. He glanced at the bell and looked at Hanuman. Maruti, the son of the Wind-God, immediately understood the Lord's intention and quickly went forward. He put his tail into the ring of the huge bell and lifted it up as easily as lifting a flower! Lo! There, trapped under the bell, were the missing vanaras! The vanaras suddenly saw light and opened their eyes. They saw the Lord of Compassion standing in front of them.

Overwhelmed at the turn of events, they all rushed forward and prostrated at the lotus feet of Sri Rama. The Lord had saved them! Sri Rama had kept his promise! The vanara-count now perfectly tallied!

Lord Rama looked around for his dear devotee. Hanuman was standing at a distance, an embodiment of humility, head bent with folded hands and eyes riveted to the Lord's feet. The shining golden bell was on his tail! Lord Rama was immensely pleased. He proclaimed, "Whosoever in future worships BHAKTA HANUMAN WITH THE BELL ADORNING HIS TAIL will be blessed with the brilliant Light of Knowledge, which alone is capable of destroying the darkness of ignorance and bestowing liberation upon the devotee; just as the vanaras were delivered from darkness of death into the blissful light of life."

"Asadhya Sadhaka Swamin, Asadhyam Tava Kim Vada; Rama Dhoota Kripasindho, Matkaryam Sadhaya Prabho!"

www.ingramcontent.com/pod-product-compliance
Ingram Content Group UK Ltd.
Pitfield, Milton Keynes, MK11 3LW, UK
UKHW021421091026
15624UKWH00010B/313

9 789390 640942